GROW UP IN GOD

A Practical Spiritual Accelerator Guide
For New Christians

(I Am Saved Now What Series)

Sherine Hemmings

Published by

DAYELight
PUBLISHERS

ISBN: 978-1-953759-36-8

_____

Table of Contents

Meet Your Acceleration Trainer

Sherine A. Hemmings is a trained marketer and honours graduate of the University of Technology, Jamaica, where she obtained an undergraduate degree in Marketing and an MBA in Entrepreneurship. She is a Product Manager with one of the largest Distributors of commercial and pharmaceutical products in Jamaica, a certified Christian Life Coach with DayeLight International, and the CEO/Founder of Kingdom Originals Jamaica, a Christian Apparel Company.

With certifications in Introduction to Hermeneutics and Homiletics from the Deeper Life School of Evangelism Jamaica, and currently a student at the WAFIF Christian College, Sherine has a passion for ministries that involve the perfecting of the saints. She now serves as an Executive Leadership Assistant to the various ministry departments at Worship & Faith International Fellowship (WAFIF).

She gave her life to Christ at age fifteen and backslid some time after. She has been through years of perishing in the world through disappointment, failure, heartache, depression, and near madness, and was finally led to discover who Jesus is, the significance of what He did for us, and this beautiful Holy Spirit who God has gifted us with to guide us through this incredibly challenging yet rewarding Christian journey. Sherine has therefore made it her mission to share with the world the message that we can be as close to God and as powerful in Him as we choose to be. The degree to which God can use us is not dependent on how much we have of Him but how much He has of us.

Dedication

I dedicate this book to the Holy Spirit, without whose wisdom and guidance this book would not have become a reality.

To my mom and dad, who gave me the faith and confidence to know in my heart that I can accomplish anything in life.

To my mentor, Bishop Courtney McLean, who became an inspiration to me from the very first moment I walked through the doors of his church, and who somehow managed to see the potential in me, even when I could not quite see it in myself.

To my faithful intercessors, my Aunts Edna and Margaret, and Cousin Nadine, who relentlessly kept me prayed up despite undergoing their own trials.

To my book coach, Crystal Daye, who was determined to become a thorn in my side until I successfully completed this book.

To my other silent but loyal cheerleaders who continually cheer me on behind the scenes despite my "underdog" status, relentlessly praying for my win; those who have continued to believe in my abilities and graciously cheer me on, even in times when failure seem sure.

To the inspiring youth of WAYACA, who kept tugging on my spirit to write this book when they confided in me even their darkest secrets and struggles in their pursuit of a victorious life in Christ.

To you, the reader, you are the ultimate reason for this book. I pray that as you scrutinize the content of these pages, your spirit will be lifted, and you will become inspired to accelerate your growth in God like never before. May you experience a new hunger and desire to get to know our glorious Creator, and may you also discover the fact that you can be as close to God as you choose to be.

2 STEPS TO ACHIEVING SPIRITUAL GROWTH FASTER

Introduction

To my newest brothers and sisters in Christ, welcome to the most amazing family you will ever be privileged to be a part of in this life: that is, the kingdom of the only true and living God. When we were born, we had no choice or say as it relates to the family we were born in. Some of us were born and raised in families and circumstances that were considered less than desirable. However, our merciful heavenly Father has given us the miraculous opportunity and choice of being reborn into His royal family through His Son, Jesus Christ, so we can have life abundantly and claim the promises of the most priceless inheritance: a happy eternal life. Hallelujah!

Congratulations on making the wise decision to choose life!

Now that you have taken this bold step, be cautioned; your journey has just begun. Many churches focus most of their efforts on leading us to salvation, and rightly so, for without it, we would be destined to an eternity that is cut off from God. However, often we operate as though salvation is a destination rather than the beginning of our journey with Christ. As a result, many new Christians tend to get stuck spiritually, while others eventually return to their old way of life because they lack the knowledge necessary for advancement in the kingdom of God. In other words, after salvation, sometimes we simply do not know what to do next.

Our goal after salvation is to grow up in God. The only way to achieve this is to pursue a real relationship with Him through His Son, Jesus Christ. One principle you must learn very quickly, if you are to have a chance at Godly success, is that spiritual growth is not accidental but intentional. It does not happen by chance; you must work for it.

This book focuses on two main steps we must take if we are to successfully reach a new level of spiritual maturity and successfully begin to grow up in God. Each step also provides simple yet practical tips and strategies that can be effortlessly applied right now to achieve the quickest results.

STEP ONE: Throw Out The Trash

Therefore, if any man be in Christ, he is a new creature: old things are passed away; behold, all things are become new.
2 Corinthians 5:17 – KJV

When we first make the decision to accept and follow Christ, we come to Him still having all our faults. As we persistently pursue a deeper knowledge of God through Christ, we are able to develop our relationship with Him and are taken through a journey of refinement and perfecting. This is where we intentionally seek to get rid of our previous sinful character to become like Jesus Christ. This process is called spiritual growth. Every Christian goes through this process after salvation for the purpose of attaining spiritual maturity. This state is reached when we start becoming more like Jesus.

Throwing out the trash is a metaphor used to describe the process of deliberately getting rid of those unnecessary and unhealthy things and habits from our old lives that pose a threat to our new walk and our ability to become like Christ. These things and habits are

15

referred to as threats because they make it hard for us to do the things that are pleasing to God. Before writing this book, I interviewed several new Christians regarding their biggest challenges to maintaining a Godly life. Their responses fell into five main categories: possessions, practices, personality, people, and pursuits. I refer to them as the five Ps. I have discovered that growth in Christ becomes possible and significantly easier when we throw out the trash in these five 'P' areas of our lives.

Chapter 1
Possessions

One of the key areas for throwing out the trash at the beginning of our Christian walk is in the area of our possessions. This involves getting rid of those material things that distract us from the things of God and achieving His purpose in our lives. Before accepting Christ as our personal Saviour, many of us owned and continually collected and invested in questionable things that gave us great pleasure but were displeasing to God. These things may have polluted our minds, thoughts and encouraged unhealthy habits that opened the door to sin in our lives. If we are to accelerate our spiritual growth, it is necessary to take an inventory of these possessions and throw them in the trash.

One day, as I lay in my bedroom, the Holy Spirit brought my attention to my bookcase. Shortly after, a question crept into my mind: Do the books in your library accurately reflect who you are as a child of God? I scanned the contents of the very full shelves and realized that out of the nearly one hundred books contained within, only about twelve were faith-based books. Every other book was a romance novel, most of which contained pages full of steamy sexual content not appropriate for a young, single Christian female at all. Most of the stories were enough to make even the most seasoned married woman blush. With that realization, suddenly, my book stand, which was once a source of great delight for me, became an object of embarrassment. I was immediately convicted. We have heard it said that "We are what we eat," but what was I feeding on? Was it healthy? Were the contents within those books feeding my spirit or corrupting my soul? Shortly thereafter, I was challenged to get rid of all that trash and replace them with faith-based books that provided keys to aiding my spiritual progress in Christ.

Later reflection revealed that every ungodly relationship I have ever been a part of was because of me chasing after the false ideal of love portrayed in the pages of those books. No wonder every romantic relationship I was ever involved in up to that point in my life ended in disappointment! It occurred to me that I had been reading books of this nature since the age of twelve. After receiving salvation at the age of fourteen years, I continued reading my novels as no one cautioned me against this unhealthy practice on my new journey. Consequently, this dictated a destructive pattern and set the tone and standard for the romantic relationships in my adult life, all because I did not throw out the trash!

Do you find yourself struggling to do the things that are pleasing to God, practice good habits, or grow spiritually as a child of God? Could it be that there may be some trash amongst your prized possessions that need to be tossed? It could be some secular books, magazines, music, movie collection, social media content, or even some immodest clothing. Regardless of what it may be, I encourage you to ask God to help you release it today. His Word says in Matthew 7:7a, "Ask, and it shall be given you" (KJV). When you do, you make it possible for Him to give you something fresh and much healthier to replace it.

Key Lesson

Complete a thorough assessment of all the regular sources of entertainment within your home or any place you spend most of your time, and dispose of those questionable items that negatively influence your ability to do the things that are pleasing to God.

Self-Evaluation

What questionable possessions am I holding on to that may be encouraging habits that are not pleasing to God?

_____

_____

_____

_____

_____

_____

_____

Self-Coaching

What strategies can you use to stay away from those possessions that may be unhealthy to your progress in growing in God?

_____

_____

_____

_____

_____

_____

Chapter 2
Practices

Now that we have gotten rid of the things (possessions) in our physical space that negatively impact our spiritual growth, it is now time to tackle those unhealthy habits that were developed as a result of having those things. Habits are those consistent practices in our lives that have become so ingrained in us that they have now shaped our lifestyle and, ultimately, our personality. When these practices result in us disobeying God, they are classified as sin. Even after accepting Christ as our Lord and Saviour, many of us still struggle with sinful habits and addictions from our past life outside of Christ. This is sometimes as a result of us holding on to those things or possessions that influenced sinful habits.

In my situation, maintaining my romance novel collection after being saved provided a constant and ever-present temptation for me to keep reading those books. This unhealthy practice subtly influenced me over time to start desiring the experiences of the characters in the books. Before I knew it, I began actively trying to live out that which I beheld in those books. This propelled me into a sinful life of fornication and, eventually, became one of the hardest sins that I have ever had to overcome. No matter what I did, a part of me continued to desire the representation of love portrayed in those books. This led me into a seriously backslidden state, and it was many years and many disappointments later before I woke up to the voice of the Holy Spirit and realized it was time to "throw out the trash."

Removing the physical temptation of possessions that encourage ungodly habits make it possible to replace these with Godly alternatives. There is an old saying that we must throw out the old to make way for the new. It becomes hard to adopt new Godly habits without getting rid of our old sinful habits. Habits, whether good or bad, affect our mental and emotional state and, ultimately, our spiritual state.

Just as garbage in our physical surroundings make it dirty, polluted, and unhygienic, so too does trash and junk in our mental space make it an unhealthy environment for us to thrive spiritually. One of the key things about junk is that it creates an attractive habitat for pests which is harmful to one's physical health. Therefore, just as we need to empty our physical garbage every day, we must also empty the trash out of our mental, emotional, and spiritual lives daily to avoid pests such as demons and Satan, who is described as the accuser of the brethren (See Revelation 12:10).

When we allow sinful habits room to grow in our lives without repenting quickly, we give Satan legal right to operate in our lives by haunting us with the guilt of our actions constantly and using his demons to afflict us with various curses such as illness, poverty and even untimely death. Once we sin, we should quickly ask for forgiveness, then put practical steps in place to avoid engaging in that sin again. It is important to acknowledge that repentance is not just asking God for His forgiveness and feeling sorry about what we have done. Rather, repentance is the act of turning away from sin and turning our minds back to Christ.

We must always have an intentional and well-thought-out plan to avoid and overcome habitual sins. This plan must, of course, include daily repentance. Just like the apostle Paul in 1 Corinthians 15:31, we should "die daily." Be encouraged; getting rid of any sinful practice is indeed possible with persistence. We just need to be intentional and serious about tossing them away like garbage.

Key Lesson

We must always have an intentional and well-thought-out plan to overcome unhealthy and sinful practices in our lives.

Self-Evaluation

What unhealthy practices have I allowed to remain in my life after accepting Christ that keeps tempting me into sin?

_____

_____

_____

_____

_____

_____

Self-Coaching

What are some of the strategies that I will use to help me break these habits?

_____

_____

_____

_____

_____

Chapter 3
Personality

The next "P" that must be addressed in our lives is the area of our personality. I know this will be incredibly hard because our personalities began to take shape inside the womb. Personality can be defined as the combination of mental and moral qualities or characteristics of an individual that form their character and make them who they are as a person. In other words, the way a person typically thinks, feels, or acts that make them different from somebody else describes their personality. Being fresh out of the world and new to salvation, it is natural that we would still have most of our worldly ways of thinking, feeling, and acting. However, if we are to successfully begin the process of spiritual growth after salvation, we must now work on getting rid of our former character (i.e., our old man) to now accommodate and take on a new personality or character (i.e., the identity of Christ).

Usually, every human being has a combination of both desirable and undesirable personality traits, some of which psychologists may argue are natural, meaning we were born with it, while others are learned as we grow up and are socialized in different environments. In this text, personality traits are described as desirable or undesirable based on their effectiveness in helping to push us toward or away from God. Therefore, our good personality traits will aid us in our efforts to successfully serve God, while the negative ones will hinder our progress in pursuing God. It is possible to have many good personality traits and just a few bad ones, but the few bad ones can cancel out the effects of the many good ones if we are not careful. This is so because negative personality traits can easily open the door to sin in our lives.

Let us take, for example, a person who has the personality trait of being easily angered. It would be possible for such an individual to become verbally and physically abusive. If he or she is unable to control that emotion over time and continues this pattern of behavior, this can lead to them taking someone else's life or even their own. Ephesians 4:26 advises us that we can be angry, but it is important not to allow that anger to lead us to sin; neither should we entertain the emotion long enough for it to lead to that. It is important for us to work on getting rid of these negative personality traits, or eventually, Satan can use them as weapons against us to create strongholds in our lives.

The key to throwing out the trash from our personality is to address the area of our thinking. This is essential because our thoughts influence our feelings, and our feelings ultimately guide our actions. Many of us, even believers who have been in the faith for a long time, suffer from a condition that is referred to as "stinking thinking." Stinking thinking speaks to frequent toxic thoughts that create an attitude centered around pessimism, negativity, fear, or unbelief. Most of us are carrying around these unpleasant thoughts that are causing us to live a defeated Christian life. Sadly, this is one of the easiest weapons the enemy uses to lead us into defeat frequently. We must start throwing out worldly thinking so we can replace it with the mind of Christ.

The moment we received salvation was the moment we invited and gave the Holy Spirit permission to dwell inside us. Therefore, because He is inside us, we now have the ability to take on the mind of Christ. We are able to take on the mind of Christ when we yield to the instructions and conviction of the Holy Spirit concerning our daily decisions and situations. The Holy Spirit is Jesus, who is God within man. So, when we hear from the Holy Spirit, we are hearing from God, and when we choose to obey the Holy Spirit, we are choosing to take up the mind of Christ already in us.

I have noticed that when we continually practice negative behaviors over time, they eventually become attitudes that frequently influence our actions and ultimately help mold our personalities. In fact, that was the case with many of the sinful practices we were encouraged to throw out in the previous chapter. The great news is: many of the negative personality traits we now identify in our lives are not natural; that is, we were not born with them. They are just bad habits that were learned, developed along the way, and embraced as being a part of us. For that reason, they can be destroyed and changed with just a bit of focused intentionality. Are you ready to throw out your stinking thinking?

Key Lesson

Throw away negative thoughts and attitudes centered around pessimism, negativity, fear, or unbelief.

Self-Evaluation

List the personality traits you believe are currently hindering you in your progress to pursuing a greater dimension in God and give an example of how one of them has hindered your spiritual growth so far.

_____

_____

_____

_____

_____

_____

_____

_____

_____

Self-Coaching

How can I help control stinking thinking from affecting my attitude?

_____

_____

_____

_____

_____

_____

_____

_____

_____

_____

Chapter 4
People

The next area for throwing out the trash may prove to be one of the most difficult but the most necessary. It involves cutting off or minimizing our interaction with people who may be toxic to our relationship with God. Some persons will have to be cut off completely based on their threat level. Sadly, sometimes, threats to our new journey in Christ may also come in the form of old, unsaved friends and acquaintances. As new-born babes in Christ, we can become spiritually stunted because of poor choices in deciding what and who we allow to remain and serve as an active and influential part in our lives. Many times, it is the people and things that we surround ourselves with that encourage sinful habits.

In my survey, recorded among the top five struggles among new converts, was peer pressure from old friends who were still in sin. One scary fact I have discovered is that it is more likely for our unsaved friends to influence us as a new Christian than it is for us to influence them. Being so new in the faith, we may lack the necessary experience to readily identify those subtle temptations designed to lure us back into sinful practices.

Picture yourself standing in a well-lit area of a large room. The side of the room opposite to where you are standing is drenched in darkness. You then hear a seemingly familiar voice calling to you from out of the depths of the darkness, but you are unable to see anything or anyone. The call gets more insistent, and the voice refers to you by name, for clearly its owner knows you and can see you quite well. Instinctively, you slowly begin to walk toward the direction of the voice and ultimately the impending darkness. Before you know it, you have walked away from the light towards the darkness. In like manner, many of us are unknowingly enticed back into sinful situations because of the influence of friends (familiar voices) that are still living in sin.

Success on this journey will require the difficult choice of sometimes having to give up those people who we love but do not serve our purpose in Christ. Matthew 19:29 reflects this quite well as it reads: "And every one that hath forsaken houses, or brethren, or sisters, or father, or mother, or wife, or children, or lands, for my name's sake, shall receive a hundredfold, and shall inherit everlasting life." (KJV).

Throughout your daily life, you will find yourself in the company of unsaved friends, family, or acquaintances. Certainly, you are not expected to just ignore and neglect your loved ones or be around just Christians all the time. However, in these situations, ensure that you make your Christian position quite clear, not by haughtily announcing that you are a Christian, but your behavior should demonstrate that you live and operate by a higher standard. Always lead by example. I like to call this: "living out loud." This way, all parties present will be mindful of what they do around you. For example, I have been engaged in conversations with coworkers on numerous occasions who have used curse words while speaking to me and have apologized to me immediately after when they remember my position. The key to avoid being negatively influenced by people can be learned from the Apostle Paul in Galatians 1:10, which is to switch your focus from pleasing people to pleasing God. The more you aim to strengthen your relationship with God, is the more your desire to please Him will increase, and your desire to please others will decrease.

Key Lesson

Stop focusing on pleasing people and start focusing on pleasing God!

Self-Evaluation

Which friends or acquaintances do you find it a challenge to maintain a Godly standard around, and why?

_____

_____

_____

_____

_____

_____

_____

Self-Coaching

How can I prevent myself from compromising my Godly standards in situations where I am around unsaved friends, family, or acquaintances?

_____

_____

_____

_____

_____

_____

Chapter 5
Pursuits

The final "P" that we must throw in the trash if we are to truly grow spiritually may be one of great controversy, especially in a world that seems so consumed by self; it is in the area of pursuits. This involves giving up personal ambitions and submitting wholeheartedly to the purpose of God for our lives. King David understood this concept quite well when he said in Psalm 27:4, "One thing have I desired of the Lord, that will I seek after; that I may dwell in the house of the Lord all the days of my life, to behold the beauty of the Lord, and to enquire in his temple." (KJV). David's one sole purpose in life was to please the Lord and remain in His presence. This one desire drove and determined almost every major pursuit of David's life.

In like manner, our lives should not be about the pursuit of our own purpose but rather the pursuit of the will of God for our lives. One of the most important things to realize when you say yes to Christ is that your life is no longer about you. It now becomes about God's purpose for you. Any spiritual advancement in the kingdom of God requires us to humbly accept that this journey is not about personal advancement but self-denial. Luke 9:23 makes this very clear when it says, "If any man will come after me, let him deny himself, and take up his cross and follow me." (KJV). This decision requires us to put aside our own personal ambitions in the pursuit of His cause. As such, even the very gifts He has placed within us must in some way be used for and to His glory. We have been called to lay down our very lives for the sake of the gospel of Jesus Christ. Ministering the gospel is about the advancement of the kingdom of God rather than the promotion of one's self-interest. The brand of the gospel is Jesus Christ, not the name of the messenger.

A few years ago, it became clear to me that I had a passion for the perfecting of the saints through the teaching of key principles in the Word of God. I was a huge admirer of the Joyce Meyer ministry and the impact she seemed to have on people's spiritual lives across the world. As such, I greatly desired a ministry like hers. I began creating vision boards using images of the audiences at her conventions and events. I would then impose an image of myself on a stage in front of her audience with the hopes that one day I too would speak in front of crowds that large. However, one day, through great conviction, the Holy Spirit had me examine my motives. Why was it so important for me to have a ministry as large as hers? What if He called to minister to only one hundred people instead of tens of thousands? Would I walk away because that was too small a number? Or what if He called me to minister through books instead of on stages? Would that be a hindrance? After being thoroughly honest with myself, I realized my motives were not one hundred percent pure. Deep down, I desired the sense of importance such a ministry would give me as it would epitomize my and the world's idealization of success. I figured it would make my parents proud and admired, especially among their peers. I became embarrassed as I thought to myself: Why wasn't the glory of God my primary motivation?"

Sadly, this is the case for many of us: our motives concerning Christ are not necessarily genuine. Child of God, I implore you to purify your motives as you move further on this journey. If we genuinely want to experience the fullness of Christ and His power, we must first allow ourselves to be fully surrendered to Him. In order to truly live, we must first fully die to ourselves. For God to fully use us, we must experience the stripping away of self. Let us, therefore, put down our personal ambitions and lay ourselves at the feet of our Saviour, Jesus Christ, acknowledging Him as Lord and Master of our lives. Accept His guidance and allow Him to lead us any way He deems suitable, living a life where we give the utmost of ourselves for God's highest glory.

Key Lesson

Purify our motives, always giving our utmost for God's highest!

Self-Evaluation

Am I truly submitted to the purpose of God for my life, or am I more driven by my own goals for my life? How so?

_____

_____

_____

_____

_____

_____

Self–Coaching

What do I believe is the will of God for my life? This is a list of four ways I can use the gifts and talents He has blessed me with to honour Him with my life.

_____

_____

_____

_____

_____

Major Section Takeaway

Do away with the Possessions, Practices, Personality, People, and Pursuits that do not serve your Godly Purpose.

STEP TWO: Feed From The Living Tree

And be not conformed to this world: but be ye transformed by the renewing of your mind, that ye may prove what is that good, and acceptable, and perfect, will of God.
(Romans 12:2 - KJV)

In Genesis 2:9, there is mention of a tree that God planted in the midst of the garden of Eden called the tree of life. The same tree is mentioned again several times in the book of Revelations. By all indication, this tree was made to give life to, improve and continuously sustain the physical life of humanity. I believe Jesus can be compared to the tree of life, for when we feed consistently upon Him through His Word, we grow spiritually and prosper. His words are life to those who find them and health to their flesh (See Proverbs 4:22). Those who believe in Him can access eternal life through Him (See John 3:16). For Jesus is life (See John 14:6 and John 1:4).

Now that we have thrown out the trash in step one; that is, purposely getting rid of those avoidable things and habits that negatively affect our new walk in Christ, it is now time to go about the process of intentionally replacing those old things and practices with new and edifying ones that will rapidly accelerate our spiritual growth and make our Christian journey a more victorious one. All of this can be described as the process of renewing one's mind, where we aim to arm ourselves with the same mind of Christ. We do so effectively by seeking after, building, and strengthening the relationship with our heavenly Father through His Word, Holy Spirit, the individuals He has specifically planted in our lives for His glory, and doing those things that He delights in. When we connect to Him in these ways, we are feeding from the Living Tree.

The proceeding chapters explain how we can successfully achieve this using a tried, tested, and proven achievement system that I have named using the acronym B.I.R.T.H. for ease of memory. This represents the following:

- Books
- Individuals
- Routine Prayer
- Time, Talent, Treasures
- Holy Ghost Dependence

This is where things get really exciting! As you read each upcoming chapter, I encourage you to pay keen attention, take notes and, most importantly, apply, apply, apply! If you correctly implement these strategies, just as the chapters suggest, you will rapidly begin to give birth to spiritual maturity. Guaranteed!

BOOKS

"Study to shew thyself approved unto God, a workman that needeth not to be ashamed, rightly dividing the word of truth."
2 Timothy 2:15 – KJV

Chapter 6
Books

Your most important goal as a new Christian should be to develop a closer relationship with God. This is achieved by actively pursuing and seeking a deeper knowledge of Him. This will be one of the biggest keys to success in your Christian journey. The Word of God in Hosea 4:6 says, "my people are destroyed for lack of knowledge." (KJV). You will find that the quality of your Christian experience will be largely affected by what you do or do not know. Therefore, it will be important to seek the right knowledge from the right sources. The first thing you will need are the right books.

Bible

As new-born babies require milk for nourishment to grow, so too will you as a new-born babe in Christ require spiritual milk for sustenance to develop spiritually. Your first priority as a new Christian is getting to know Jesus Christ for yourself; that is, who He is, what He teaches, what He has done for you, the significance of what He has done for you, and what He expects from you. The best way to access this information is from the Word of God; that is, the Bible, which is the inspired Word of God and the foundational manual for victorious Christian living. This book, in addition to being the bestselling book of all time according to the Guinness World Records, also provides some vital principles necessary for persons who have just begun to seek a real relationship with God.

However, I know, as a new convert, reading the Bible can seem very intimidating. Nevertheless, there are ways to make this process way easier and less daunting. A few years ago, in my desperation to know God and His Word, I stumbled on an effective yet simple five-step strategy that worked remarkably well for me that I want to share with you. I am confident that if applied, it will work wonders for you too. Follow the following five keys step by step and begin to transform your relationship with our Heavenly Father and jumpstart your spiritual growth.

Five Simple Keys to Mastering Personal Bible Study for New Converts

- **Set the Atmosphere/Space** – Intentionally set a time and create a space where you can quietly and calmly read and process the scriptures in private. Do not get too caught up in trying to find the perfect space. You can use almost any area as your own personal sanctuary, as long as it is quiet, offers privacy, and enables you to concentrate. For me, this is my bedroom, but for you, it may be your car, closet, bathroom, or even your roof. Yes, I know, doing your personal Bible study on your roof may sound a bit crazy, but it used to be a great quiet place for me until my neighbors began to raise pigeons.

Tip: Ensure that the area you choose is clean and clutter-free because clutter can be quite a distraction. For example, when doing my personal Bible study in my bedroom, I find myself quite distracted if I have unfolded laundry or personal items lying around and out of place. Instead of meditating on the scripture, I find myself thinking, "Oh, Lord, I really should make some time to put the laundry away" or "Oh my, I need to get this room in order." I have learned that the state of your physical surrounding can be an indication of your spiritual state.

- **Expect Revelation** – When preparing to read the Word of God, we must also prepare our hearts with the expectation to hear from the Lord through His Word. There is a common myth that only particular people such as prophets, spiritual leaders, famous televangelists, Bible study teachers, etc., can hear from God. This is absolutely not true! You do not need a Bible school degree to have a genuine relationship with God. You can open up the Bible yourself and the Holy Spirit can bring light to the scriptures to provide reassurance, security, clarity and open the eyes of your understanding and speak to you through His Word. I used to eagerly follow men of God claiming to be prophets fervently, waiting to hear a word from God, when the whole time God was fervently waiting to share a word with me from His holy scriptures. We do not need to always wait on someone else to spoon-feed us the Word of God. We need to strategically position ourselves to hear the voice of God by intentionally seeking Him out in His Word. Revelation comes through relationship. The more we seek to establish a relationship with God by getting to know Him better daily through His Word, is the more about Himself that He will eventually reveal to us. Being a new convert is no excuse to forever rely on someone else to spoon-feed you the truth of God's Word. You have the privilege to go to God through His Word and hear Him for yourself. When engaging in personal Bible study, it is essential that you strategically position yourself spiritually and physically to hear from God. Come with a heart of expectation to hear from God through His Word (spiritual position) and arm yourself with a pen, notebook, and dictionary, preferably a Bible dictionary to be used in your quiet space (physical position). If you do not own one, simply go to Google's search engine and find one. My favourite one to use online is the King James Bible Dictionary.

- **Select a Verse or Passage of Scripture** – Now one of the greatest pieces of advice I can give here from experience is to never try to finish the chapter in a rush. Take each verse apart slowly, word by word, line by line, paying special attention to vocabulary, parts of speech, words beginning with capital and common letters, past and present tense, context, etc. Use your dictionary to find the meaning of significant words and phrases that may be new or unclear to you. Look at what the text is saying, then summarize and rephrase using words that you find easier to understand without changing the original meaning. Reread your summary aloud several times, meditate and think upon it for an extended period of time.

- **Pinpoint and Highlight the Spiritual Principles in the Text** – As you review your summary, and begin thinking about it, ask the following questions:

- What does this verse mean?
- What is this scripture revealing to me about God's personality?
- What pleases and what displeases Him?
- What will He permit, and what will He not permit?
- What is He commanding me to do in this scripture?
- What is He warning me about?

While pondering the above questions, just patiently wait on the Holy Spirit to reveal some insight He wants you to know concerning the scripture under study. The answers to these questions will give you an awareness of the character of God. When we begin to understand God's character, it becomes easier to identify things, people, and behaviours contrary to God's nature. This enables us to readily identify false teachers and wayward doctrines. Recognizing the character of God also makes it incredibly easier for us to identify the voice of the enemy, especially when he tries to deceive us. Readily identifying the voice of the enemy and walking contrary to that voice is a major step toward spiritual maturity!

- **Search Yourself** – Begin to examine your life and see how well your life measures up with the character of God and what He expects of you based on His Word. Wait! Do not panic! This exercise is not intended to discourage but to encourage us to address the areas that may need lots of work. God's Word is not meant to embarrass us but to provide protection, correction, and direction. When we assess ourselves in this way, we enable the Holy Spirit to shine His glorious light into the dark areas of our lives. When the Word of God begins to shine light on us, things become exposed, such as our innermost thoughts, desires, and motives (those things within us that do not resemble Christ). Understandably, many times, most of what is exposed may be unpleasant. After all, sin is ugly. This is good though, for it allows us to see ourselves for who we are and provides us the opportunity to repent and seek corrective behaviour. The psalmist wrote, "Thy word is a lamp unto my feet and a light unto my path." (Psalm 119:105 - KJV). It reveals wrong mindsets, that is, wrong ways of thinking. Knowing the Word of God without applying it to our lives is pointless. The Word of God provides sustenance for us to withstand the wiles of the devil. If we have no sustenance, then rest assured, we will crumble under pressure. Without the nourishment of God's Word, it is impossible for us to overcome temptation or bear the weight of adversity. It provides the necessary strength that enables us to press on in the will of God. Remember, the journey to perfection (spiritual maturity) is an ongoing one, not an overnight process. The cry of our hearts when reading the Word of God should be that of Psalm 139:23-24, "Search me, O God, and know my heart: try me, and know my thoughts: And see if there be any wicked way in me, and lead me in the way everlasting." (KJV).

Four Extra Super Helpful Tips for Reading the Bible When You Have No Clue Where to Start!

In the initial stages of being a young convert, awkwardly trying to navigate my way through the pages of the Bible, I had no plan and no clue what I was doing. However, I kid you not, in those times, in my little private, quiet and secluded space, God met me halfway. It was through consistently practicing studying the Bible by myself during my designated quiet times that my relationship with God began to bloom. As this began to happen, I found that my personality began to change for the better, and I began to accelerate spiritually, especially as I began to take on more of the image of Christ. It happened for me, and it can certainly happen for you!

My experience has taught me that one of the major secrets to accelerating quickly as a new convert is simply to begin to faithfully meet with God regularly through His Word. The following basic techniques helped me to effectively study the Bible as a new convert and are still my go to strategy for reading the scriptures up to this very day. I pray that as you start your own spiritual journey, may these practices help to accelerate you spiritually ten times faster!

- **Use an Easy-to-Read Translation**. Reading the Bible can be very intimidating, especially if you try reading a King James version. Help! Nevertheless, there are ways to make this process way easier and less daunting. I strongly recommend using and starting with a Bible translation that is easy to understand but credible in terms of its correctness to the original text of the Bible.

- **Choose a Starting Point Based on Your Current Needs as a New Believer.** Do not feel obligated to start reading from the beginning (Genesis). As a newbie in Christ, I greatly recommend you start your Bible study journey by seeking to learn about and fully understand who you have committed your life to (Jesus), why it is important to do so, what He did for you and what He expects from you in return. When I was a spiritually malnourished babe in Christ seeking sustenance,

I quickly discovered that not only did the first part of the New Testament known as the Gospels (Matthew, Mark, Luke and John) give a thorough account of the life and ministry of Jesus Christ, His purpose and His teachings, but it was also very easy to understand in comparison to most other books in the Bible, especially those found in the Old Testament. As such, these books made Christ more real to me and enabled me to relate to Him in a more personal way. The book of John was particularly enlightening in revealing to me the truth of who Jesus is and helping me to understand His sovereignty. When it comes on to learning the new, appropriate, and required behaviors of a child of God, then I have found the book of James to be most helpful, clear, and easily applicable. In seeking to develop the kind of faith that powers miracles, reading a chapter of the book of Acts every day is priceless.

- **Gather Essential Tools.** I recommend starting with a few simple essentials such as a good Study Bible in an easy-to-understand translation. I have found those with maps, notes, and cross-references that explain historical and cultural backgrounds to be quite helpful. This enables us to better understand the context in which the particular text was written. Understanding context makes us more likely to accurately interpret what the biblical writer is saying. Always study with a pen and notebook to summarize the passage of scripture under study, pull out key principles, and record the answers to your application questions. Ensure to utilize a Bible dictionary to shine light on those words and phrases you do not understand. Let us face it, many of us are intimidated by reading the Bible because some of the words and phrases seem complicated to understand. Do not get flustered trying to figure out the meaning of a word; rather utilize your Bible dictionary or online Bible dictionaries such as kingjamesbibledictionary.com or BibleGateway.com. Doing this will provide you with a better understanding of the words and phrases as well as shed some light as to the meaning in regards to the culture during the time highlighted by the text. Please also read the verses surrounding the passage to get more information concerning the passage of study. If you do not, you may risk incorrectly interpreting what the text means.

- **Start Small/Quality Over Quantity** – My simplest but probably greatest advice is to start off small, choosing to study smaller bits of scripture at a time. Do not be in a haste to finish reading the entire Bible without understanding. Take each verse bit by bit, apply the five *Simple Keys to Mastering Personal Bible Study for New Converts* and prepare to be amazed at the revelation that comes. There is no magic formula when studying the Word of God. However, there is one main ingredient that I know works every time; that is consistency! "Then said Jesus to those Jews which believed on him, If ye continue in my word, then are ye my disciples indeed." (John 8:31-32 – KJV).

New believers, I encourage you to develop a delight for the Word of God as this will be the foundation of all your successes in Christendom (See Joshua 1:8). According to Ephesians 6:12, we are all engaged in a spiritual battle, so it is necessary for us to equip ourselves with the appropriate dress and artilleries. The Bible is one of the most vital and lethal weapons for every Christian. It prepares and builds us up for battle and is referred to as the sword of the Spirit. Knowing when and how to wield this sword will give us victory over the enemy. It is not enough to just read the Word of God; we must learn it and apply it. Having a weapon in the midst of war without using it, while under the enemy's attack, is of no benefit to us. The benefits to studying and applying God's Word are numerous and powerful. However, we can only obtain its full benefits and accelerate spiritual growth when we study it, meditate upon it, consistently declare it, obey it, pray with it, and apply it to every area of our lives.

Tip: Program your lives around the studying of His Word, rather than trying to squeeze it into your hectic schedule.

Faith-Building Books

One of the most helpful tools I used as a baby Christian to assist my spiritual growth was that of faith-building books written by authentic Christian authors who held true and uncompromising to the Word of God. This is why starting by reading the Bible as a young Christian is essential as it helps us to measure the message of other authors against the Word of God. It helps us to readily identify flaws in their doctrine. I advise young Christians to be especially cautious when reading some of these books as many of the doctrines contained within are seriously flawed but not easily identifiable. However, many of them offer great insights into the Christian journey, and you are able to benefit from the experiences of those who started the journey long before us. It also provides a sense of comfort and increases your faith, realizing that others have also gone through similar struggles that you may be experiencing during the journey but then overcame.

Tip: Join a Bible-believing church.

I cannot emphasize enough the importance of being a part of a Bible-believing church that loves the Word of God and uses the truth of God's Word as the standard for how it operates and how its members behave. This is a big part of what will help keep us accountable when we are tempted to slip.

All that is recommended in this chapter may seem like a lot of reading, but, believe me, you can do it! It is worth it!

Prayer

Open my eyes, oh LORD, that I may behold wondrous things out of Thy law. Teach me to meditate upon Thy precepts and have respect unto Your ways. Give me a new delight for Your Word so that it may never depart out of my mouth, but I shall meditate upon it day and night and work to obey all that is therein so I may make my way prosperous and have good success. Amen!

INDIVIDUALS

He that walketh with wise men shall be wise: but a
companion of fools shall be destroyed.
Proverbs 13:20 – KJV

Chapter 7
Individuals

The second letter, 'I,' in the acronym B.I.R.T.H. refers to individuals, which is a very important contributor to spiritual growth. The speed at and degree to which we grow in the faith is greatly influenced by the quality of the individuals we choose to associate with frequently. Therefore, our level of fellowship with other individuals can either propel our growth in the faith, slow it down or keep us stunted.

As an infant born into a new family, we require the companionship and the friendship of our brothers and sisters in Christ. This relationship is essential to our learning and development during this Christian journey. The sibling bond will help to properly socialize us into the acceptable ways and customs of the family as well as teach us how to successfully cope with this new world into which we have now entered. This is of great importance at this point of our walk because it provides the necessary support we need as new-borns and creates an atmosphere for learning and protection. Each individual in the body of Christ has been blessed with different but definite special gifts for the purpose of advancing the kingdom of God. Our gifts were also designed to complement each other's gifts in the kingdom (See Romans 12:4-6). Each of us have important teachings to share with each other, which will enable us to grow spiritually. Coming together allows us to teach each other things that are valuable to successfully becoming like Christ.

We will need four main types of individuals during this time: **mentors, intercessors, accountability partners, and Christian friends.** A mentor can be described as an individual who takes a special interest in helping someone else grow and successfully develop mastery in a particular area. Christian mentors are very important to our journey because they usually have the information, revelation, and experience (knowledge) we need to be successful on our journey. Such individuals are mature Christians who have moral and spiritual authority based on their relationship with God. They are also men and women of great integrity who are rooted, grounded, and fruitful in the Word of God and can teach us and wash us in the Word. Examples of such mentors would be our pastors, bishops, etc.; those who instruct us in the Word of God. This person should inspire us to want more of God and climb higher in Him.

In the most basic of terms, an intercessor is someone who prays on behalf of someone else, particularly when that person may not be in a position to pray for themselves for some reason. I cannot say this enough, but all new converts need at least one intercessor. Once you have truly committed to a life of serving Christ, you have successfully made the devil's hitlist as you have now become a potential threat to his kingdom. Therefore, he will make it his mission to take you out. This is called spiritual warfare. The first place he usually seeks to attack us is in our minds, especially through our thoughts. He aims to fill us with doubt and fear. We, therefore, need individuals who are willing to break the bows of his efforts through prayer by consistently keeping us before the Lord, petitioning to Him on our behalf, and requesting protection over our mind, will, and emotions. During this journey, you will find that many of our victories will come through persistent prayer for the fervent prayer of a righteous man availeth much.

The third influential and valuable type of individual necessary at this stage of your walk is an accountability partner. This is a person who consistently makes themselves available to give a listening ear concerning the things that are happening in our lives and dedicate themselves to providing well-needed reassurance, constructive criticism, caution, advice, and prayer accordingly. They hold us responsible for the things we should and should not do. Such individuals are vital to our growth as Christians, for they act as both law enforcement, inspecting to see if we are moving in accordance to God's will, cautioning and calling us out when we fall out of line, and a medical practitioner checking the status of our spiritual health. As a result, they are great for helping us stay on track in our Christian walk, preventing us from falling into sin, providing objectivity, and encouraging us (we all need a cheerleader).

Christian friends are those other children of God in our lives who function as blood relatives. These people constantly remind us that we are not alone, especially in difficult times. We all experience challenging periods in our lives when we feel hurt, sad, and discouraged for whatever reason. During such seasons, it is easy to experience cynicism concerning God. However, when we have good Christian friends in our lives, they help lift us out of the misery with their dependable presence and through their consistent encouragement. I have found that God seems to work through and equip these individuals with exactly what we need to help us effectively get through gloomy times. They always seem to know the right thing to say for that time, or it could just be through the comfort of their presence. Through everything, these individuals are always able to help us keep our eyes on God despite the chaos around us.

There is power in people, particularly believers, when we fellowship together. No wonder the enemy tries to isolate us before he tries to destroy us; that is, get us away from people, into a place where we are alone and, thus, vulnerable. For this reason, offence is one of the weapons of mass destruction that he uses against Christians. When we become offended, we seek to disassociate ourselves from those who have offended us. Young Christians tend to be particularly vulnerable to this as we lack the experience and maturity necessary to quickly identify this trick. New Christians must be especially wary of this. There is power in numbers. One can chase a thousand, but two can put ten thousand to flight. Notice in the temptation of Eve and Jesus, Satan chose to approach each of them when they were alone and seemingly vulnerable. Never isolate yourself as a new Christian by making the mistake of thinking worshipping on your own alone at home is enough. The Bible encourages us to forsake not the assembly.

Prayer

Heavenly Father, complete my joy by surrounding me with the right people who are filled with Your love, being in full unity and of one mind. For Your Word says that where two or three are gathered in Your name, there You are among them. May we sharpen each other as iron sharpens iron. As I stand unified with the destiny helpers You have placed in my life, may we have a good reward for our labour. If one be cast down, may we lift up each other and may our unity strengthen us to withstand and resist the enemy; for a threefold cord is not quickly broken. Amen.

ROUTINE PRAYER

He that dwelleth in the secret place of the most high shall abide under the shadow of the Almighty.
Psalm 91:1 - KJV

Chapter 8
Routine Prayer

Need a word from God, but unsure of what to do?
Draw nigh to Him, and He will draw nigh to you.
No fancy words or eloquence needed to start.
Just a willing soul and a yielded heart.
It's as clear as day; even a blind man can see.
We can be as close to God as we choose to be.

Seek Him early, in the wee hours before the break of day.
Talk to Him, then listen carefully to what He has to say.
To hear Him, be still, listen and hear Him speak.
Don't get anxious; relax, for His strength is made perfect where we are weak.
In these moments, be equipped with pen and paper;
So you can recall all the things He said later.

When it is our turn to speak, He will anoint our lips.
For whom He has called, He certainly equips.
In the depths of your heart, may there always be a deep yearning
For increased wisdom and sharpened discerning.
Bask in His glory and wait for the outpouring.

For miracles happen when we grab the wings of the morning.

Written by Sherine Hemmings

We have often heard it said that the "Secret to our success is hidden in our daily routine." Routine can be described as those practices, behaviors, or habits that we repeat each day, so they have unconsciously become a part of us and who we are. The crucial thing to know about these daily habits is that they have the power to determine if we live a victorious or defeated life. One such habit is that of prayer. This should be one of your first disciplined steps towards establishing intimacy with God. Prayer can be described as the act of communicating and fellowshipping with God, whether impulsively or purposefully as a form of worship, adoration, supplication, confession, and thanksgiving.

As a new convert, you will quickly discover that daily prayer will be an essential part of our quiet time with God and one of the most important ingredients for our spiritual growth. As we grow more and more in the faith, we learn that it is necessary to keep our spiritual battery charged. When we rely on our own might, it becomes quite easy to run out of steam. However, God reminds us that it is not by might, nor by power but by His Spirit that we are able to overcome any mountain that stands before us.

Prayer helps to empower us spiritually so we can effectively demonstrate the power of God, especially when we are evangelizing to others. Consistent prayer helps us to maintain and grow our connection with God through His Holy Spirit.

Psalm 91:1 suggests that as long as we make our dwelling in the secret place of the Most High a lifestyle, then we will be able to experience a lifetime of protection from our heavenly Father. Additionally, Proverbs 8:34-35 says, "Blessed is the man that heareth me, watching daily at my gates, waiting at the posts of my doors. For whosoever findeth me findeth life, and shall obtain favour of the Lord." (KJV – emphasis mine). This also implies that a Godly, daily routine, namely one that includes prayer, has highly beneficial rewards for us. As believers, we carry the presence of God through a lifestyle of constant fellowship with Him and not by an occasional visit. It is our relationship with God that gives us authority and power to overrule the forces of darkness.

Our daily habit of fellowshipping with God will ultimately determine if we grow and how quickly we grow in spiritual maturity. How valuable is a victorious

Christian life to you? Are you tired of living a life of defeat and discouragement with little to no progress? Are you ready to adopt a lifestyle that will rapidly build your spiritual strength, protect you from the wiles of the enemy, enable you to live a victorious Christian life, and ultimately make you a more effective Christian? Implement the suggested *Routine Prayer Plan* below that changed my life to help keep you grounded, safe from the onslaught of the enemy, and propel you into success.

Set A Daily Appointment With God And Keep it

Schedule specific times of the day to meet with, worship, and talk to God in private for a set amount of time each day. I recommend a minimum of thirty minutes to start. This should be at the same time each day for the same amount of time so the habit of intentional prayer can be developed. If we are to experience any significant advancement in the Christian faith, we must be intentional about making God a priority in our lives; that is, we must simply choose to pray. Therefore, just as we make time within our day to spend time with family and friends who are important to us, so too should we be deliberate about making time to fellowship with God. Daniel 6:10 says that Daniel kneeled three times a day, prayed, and gave thanks before God. Intentionally scheduling set times of the day to meet with God in prayer ensures we do not squeeze God into our busy schedules but rather make Him a priority by scheduling the other areas of our lives around our prayer time with Him. Let us, therefore, change our routine so that we may become dedicated to prayer. Such behavior honours God, thus creating the opportunity for God to also honour us (See 1 Samuel 2:30).

Disconnect to Reconnect

Once we have determined a set time, we now need to identify a set meeting place that will allow solitude. I have a Finance Manager who places a "Do not Disturb" sign on her door once every month during payroll. Everyone who sees that sign on the firmly closed door knows to absolutely avoid interrupting her, unless the building is burning down. In like manner, we have to be very protective and deliberate about our alone time with God. As such, I recommend putting away our cell phones, asking immediate family for uninterrupted privacy, and finding a place that offers both seclusion and quietness. This can be somewhere in your house—whether a room or closet—in your yard, a private park, or in the hills; basically, anywhere from noise, prying eyes, and ears. For me, this place is my bedroom.

Some persons have a reasonably sized closet space that works well for them. Wherever works best for you, as long as it enables you to disconnect temporarily. This momentary isolation will allow you to put away and shut out external distractions for the purpose of giving God your full attention and re-establishing effective communication and fellowship with Him. I have found that reverent stillness before the Lord attracts His presence; that is, when we quiet our minds before Him by drowning out distracting thoughts and interruptions within our environment, it becomes easier for God to welcome us into the depths of His presence. Disconnecting to reconnect is even more essential because Jesus also practiced it. Scriptures such as Mark 1:35 supports that Jesus made it a frequent practice to isolate Himself in a solitary place where He could be away from the crowd in order to pray to His Father.

Rise Early to Meet Him

I have found early mornings, before dawn, to be one of the most conducive and effective times of the day to seek fellowship with the Lord. This is usually between 3 AM and 5:30 AM. There is less likelihood of distractions from members of the household, nature, or from vehicles passing by, thus facilitating an atmosphere for focus. Some of the greatest men in the Bible made a habit of practicing this very powerful Biblical principle. Job would rise early in the morning and offer the Lord burnt offerings on behalf of each of his children (See Job 1:4-5). This shows that rising early to offer our sacrifice of prayer and praise to the Lord can be a tool of protection for ourselves and our loved ones. Jesus also habitually rose while it was still dark and prayed privately (See

Mark 1:35). We see where this practice made His ministry very powerful. He never had to pray to cast out demons; He just commanded them out.

King David says in Psalm 5:3, "In the morning, LORD, you hear my voice; in the morning I lay my requests before you and wait expectantly." (NIV). David was not only confident that God heard his voice when he prayed in the early morning, but he keenly expected that God would respond to his prayer. Rising early seemed to have been a routine practice for King David as he made his intentions clear to deliberately rise early to seek God because his soul was thirsty for Him (See Psalm 63:1). This suggests that seeking God early in the morning can refresh our minds, will, and emotions.

I always warn new believers against being spiritually passive because the moment we accept Christ as Lord, we seem to automatically make the devil's hit list. Satan makes a career out of waging spiritual war against the children of God. Early morning prayer is a spiritual offensive weapon that allows us to effectively wage war against the enemy. It also enables us to command the outcome of our day by preparing us against any potential demonic attacks. It can equip us to resist temptation, triumph over the devil, and make us more resilient toward any challenging situation that we may face throughout the course of the day.

Pray Scripture

In the beginning, when talking to God, many of us tend to feel intimidated at first. In fact, we feel unsure as to what to say to this great and awesome God. Therefore, what was intended to be a beautiful prayer time with God may become awkward, with you sometimes eventually falling asleep. Think of an uncomfortable first date. You do not know the other person well and have to be scrambling for conversation. Do not be discouraged if this happens; you are not alone. It is perfectly normal. Believe me, I have been there. However, I discovered that the greatest key to overcoming this is to pray using the Word of God; that is, praying the Word of God back to Him. When we take a verse from scripture and personalize it, it takes on a new level of meaning and power to us. It has the ability to encourage your soul and spirit and increases the intensity of our prayer because our confidence is also stirred. 1 John 5:14-15 says, "and this is the confidence that we have in Him, that if we ask any thing according to His will, he heareth us: And if we know that He hear us, whatsoever we ask, we know that we have the petitions that we desired of Him." (KJV). Praying scripture puts us in a position to ask according to God's will and have the confidence that He hears us and will respond to those requests. This practice is also a way of submitting ourselves to God and allowing Him to complete a perfect work in us.

When reading scripture, many times, we come upon verses that grab our attention, whether because of its profoundness or because they may be relevant to a situation we are going through. This is not an accident or a coincidence. The Holy Spirit, many times, bring these verses to our attention so they speak to our spirit man. I encourage you to always write these down and utilize them when praying. Praying these verses may just be one of the steppingstones to victory in whatever situation you may be going through. (See the prayers at the end of chapters 6 to 10, which are examples of personalized prayers from scripture).

Set the Mood With a Heart of Gratitude

When we reflect on the good things God has done for us, it prepares our hearts for worship and prayer. In many of King David's prayers, he made it a habit to express thanks to the Lord (See Psalm 34:1-3). In the silence, begin to think upon the ways that Jesus has made Himself personal to you. What has He ever done for you that makes you extremely thankful? Did He heal you from a terrible illness? Did He come through for you during a seemingly hopeless situation? Did He rescue you from a potentially harmful situation? Did He provide for you during a time of lack? In what way has God made Himself real or known to you? Begin to thank Him aloud for every one of these individual moments in which He has come through for you. You will find that the more you begin to thank Him for these things, the more things you will find to thank Him for. Do not panic if you begin to get emotional. Just relax and allow the Spirit of God to be free. You will soon find that as you begin to express gratitude, that worship and prayer will begin to flow easily.

Tip: Always remember that gratitude is an essential part of prayer.

Take Time to Listen

Always remember that prayer is a two-way conversation. Therefore, once we have our time to speak to Him, we must allow time for God to speak to us. This requires us to listen quietly in the silence and meditate on Him and His Word after we have prayed. Ensure to have a notepad and a pen ready. This is the posture of expectation and an act of demonstrated faith. Being equipped shows that you are expecting to hear from God. You may not hear an audible voice, but you may begin to sense His voice in your spirit. This may be in the form of particular instructions; you may sense that the Lord wants you to do something, or He may place a particular verse of scripture in your heart. How do we know we are hearing from God? Whatever you hear should always be supported by scripture. The Lord will not instruct you to do anything that is outside of His will.

Tips on How to Pray When You do not Know What to Say

1. Go to prayer with a plan. Write down those things, people, and situations in your daily life that you wish to have a heart-to-heart with God about.

2. Find scriptures that address or give counsel concerning these things, people, and situations.

3. Personalize the selected scriptures by applying them to your situation and praying accordingly.

Bonus Tips:

- In addition to engaging in intentional prayer, also practice spontaneous prayer throughout the day.

- Do not get discouraged if you miss your appointment with God one day. Just pick up where you left off previously.

Prayer

My Lord and my God, give me the grace to always pray and never to faint. May I never be anxious for anything, but in everything by prayer, supplication and thanksgiving make my requests known to You and, in turn, may You grant me the peace of God that passes all understanding. Hear my supplications, oh Lord. Hear from heaven, Your dwelling place, and when You hear, forgive. Amen.

TIME
TALENT TREASURES

For unto every one that hath shall be given, and
he shall have abundance: but from him that hath
not shall be taken away even that which he hath.
Matthew 25:29 – KJV

Chapter 9
Time Talent Treasures

Now that you have become an authentic member of the family of God, your entire outlook on life and the purpose for living will have to change. One such perspective concerns how you invest your time, talents, and treasures. Consider yourself now as a kingdom investor; that is, one who consistently uses his/her God-given resources to advance the kingdom of God. Since you do not belong to yourself and no longer to the devil but you have been bought with a price; that is, by the blood of Jesus, your entire life's purpose is now wrapped up in God. You now exist for His glory and His honour.

Time

In this context, time can be described as the period in which we have to accomplish our God-given purpose here on earth. Whatever consumes your time is an indication as to what you consider valuable. You can begin to invest your time in doing things that bring glory to God. One of the easiest and most practical ways to do this as a new believer is to get involved in serving at your church. This is a great way to accelerate you spiritually because serving helps to develop and bring out the fruit of the Spirit within us, which is love, joy, peace, gentleness, longsuffering, etc. (See Galatians 5:22). Find an area of ministry that you believe you can really add value and get involved. I recommend choosing an area that may be connected to a skill or natural ability that you have. Let us say you have a naturally warm smile and welcoming personality; you would be a great fit for the ushering ministry. If you have a burden for helping the less fortunate, get involved in your church's Benevolence Department. A great area to serve if you are naturally gifted in teaching and great with children is that of children's Sunday school. These are just a few examples of ways to use your time to honour God.

Talent

In scripture, the use of the word "Talent" usually refers to a monetary currency. However, in this guide, talent will be used to refer to those unique abilities and capabilities that God has placed within us for the purpose of accomplishing the distinct assignment He has given us here on earth. As a new believer, you may not yet know what your unique assignment is. However, your responsibility is to develop your God-given talents, and as you do so, the Lord can reveal this to you. Once you avail yourself and your talent to be used by the Lord, He will equip you.

When I discovered that I had an aptitude for teaching, I decided to attend Bible School with the hope of guiding others in the Word of God. With every new thing I learned, I would practice by teaching family and friends. The next thing I knew, I began receiving invitations to share the Word of God in my Youth Church, my family church, other churches, and at work functions. Most times, despite being prepared, I would be quite nervous and become unsure of exactly what to say. However, each time the Lord would build on the little I had and fill my mouth with what to say. Just like that, because I availed myself, doors began to open for me to advance the kingdom of God by sharing His Word in different forums.

Your talent may be different; you may have many or just one. Whatever God has given you, just build on it. The more you use these skills is the better you get at them.

Again, one of the quickest and easiest ways to develop your talents is through service in church. You can also pursue more formal avenues of training that will enhance your talent, such as short courses. Many of these are readily accessible online at very reasonable prices. If you are unable to enroll in a paid course at this time, not a problem. Try YouTube university. It is free!

Treasure

Finally, we must seek to honour God with our wealth (finances and possessions). Generally, this is a touchy subject, but you will quickly learn that passing the money test is also crucial in accelerating spiritually. It is a reflection of the degree of your spiritual growth.

Child of God, understand this clearly: money in and of itself has no power. It cannot act on its own. Money does what we command it to do. In other words, for money to work or be useful in any way, it requires man to give it an assignment. 1 Corinthians 10:31 says that whether we eat or drink, or whatever we do, do it all to the glory of God. This includes the way we use our money. Our aim as children of God is to use our money to accomplish Godly objectives. This requires us to give our money a Godly assignment.

In fact, the way we use our money can be viewed as a form of worship. Our willingness to invest our wealth in the work of God demonstrates that we honour and value Him above everything else. Many times, we become so fearful about parting with our money that we neglect to bless others and, in so doing, we miss out on the blessings of God in our lives. Proverbs 11:24 says, "One man gives freely, yet he grows richer, while another withholds what he should give and end up suffering want." (ESV). When we give freely, it will be given back to us in multiplied measure (See Luke 6:38).

Worshiping God with our money requires us to receive, utilize and give up our money and assets in such a way that shows that God has the highest worth, significance, and importance in our lives, not money and things!

Here are four simple ways I began to honour the Lord with my treasures, and He honoured me back big time! It worked for me, and just watch it work for you too!

1. Develop a Godly and Positive Attitude Towards Giving

Giving can be hard, especially when things seem tight financially. However, we must give with enthusiasm, for the power of giving lies within the heart with which it was given. 2 Corinthians 9:7 says we should make up in our own hearts what we want to give, of our own free will, not unwillingly or under force, for God loves a cheerful giver. Mark 12:41-44 gives an account of a poor widow who gave to the treasury two mites as she did not have much compared to other rich givers who were able to contribute much. However, Jesus considered her contribution to be way more significant than that of the rich givers because they gave out of their abundance, but the widow gave out of her little, thus making her giving a sacrificial offering. Jesus acknowledged her sacrifice.

We need to develop a Godly and positive attitude towards giving. We must first and foremost acknowledge that it is God who gives us the power to gain wealth (See Deuteronomy 8:18). Therefore, He expects us to use the earthly treasures He has blessed us with for His glory. We do this by using our wealth to enrich the kingdom of God and help others.

A great place to start practicing our giving is by contributing to the place we receive our spiritual food (church); however, this is not where we should stop.

We should use our wealth to help and serve others, especially those who may have significantly less than we do.

I must say, initially, I struggled in some areas of giving, especially in the times when it seemed like I did not have a lot to share. However, in those moments when I decided to extend myself despite the little I had, the LORD has continually proven Himself faithful. I guarantee that this is an amazing way to experience miracles and build your faith rapidly in God.

2. Begin to Tithe

Tithe refers to the tenth part of anything. Therefore, tithing from our finances would require us to give to the LORD the first 10% of any income we receive. This can be in the form of wages received from work performed or income received as a gift. In Malachi 3:10, we are encouraged by God to bring all our tithes into His house so there will be supply there. In so doing, it gives us the opportunity to prove and trust God to bless us abundantly.

Tithing should never be considered a burden but must be viewed and treated as an expression of honour and commitment to God. It demonstrates that our trust and hope for provision is in God and not in our money, and trains us in the habit of putting God first (See Deuteronomy 14:23). This is why I practice taking out my tithe first out of any income I receive before using it to do anything else.

When I was first introduced to the principle of tithing, I was very unsure about it. In fact, I was convinced that it was just an outdated practice that was not necessary for Christians today. As such, I chose to ignore it. However, seemingly out of nowhere and quite frequently, I began to stumble on and notice articles, books, and videos that explained the importance of tithing. I could no longer ignore it; I became convicted. One month I decided to try it and convinced myself that I did not notice anything spectacular. Nevertheless, I continued to tithe in an attempt to develop the habit because I began encouraging myself to view giving to the LORD more as a privilege and not an obligation. I was aiming to develop a Godly and positive attitude towards giving. Soon after, I began to notice that I was no longer caught up in the anxious countdown to payday at the end of each month. In fact, for many months, payday would pass without me even noticing. Without realizing, I was no longer living from paycheck to paycheck!

I continued to pay my tithe faithfully for months. However, one month I experienced some unforeseen and unplanned expenses. For the first time since starting my new tithing habit, I began having doubts, so I reasoned with God. I said, "Lord, I am having a serious difficulty paying my tithes this month due to all these unplanned expenses. Is it okay if I skip this month?" I did not hear the response in an audible voice, but I kept feeling a constant impression on my spirit to pay my tithes and prove God. With a heavy heart, I decided to obey what I felt in my spirit, but I spoke to God first. I said, "Lord, I will do what I believe You want me to do but prove to me that giving tithe to You is necessary." People of God, I kid you not, that same week I accidentally reversed into the back of a very expensive car while trying to get out of a very small parking lot. In fact, the owner of the car later told me that the cost of one of his car lights could buy my car twice. The sound of the collision was so loud, I sat in the car sobbing uncontrollably, refusing to alight from the vehicle to investigate the damage. The sound was so frightening that people came running from all over, including a coworker of mine. She was the one who actually went to examine the possible damage. Seeing her face on her return to my car window, I began to wail loudly. She had a look of utter disbelief on her face, and I interpreted it to mean things were really bad. She tried to convince me to come out and look, and I refused. Instead, I sat in the car gripping the steering wheel and wailing loudly while a crowd gathered. She kept saying to me, "Sherine, you really have to come see; this is unbelievable!" Eventually, I found the courage to step out and look. There was not even a scratch on either my car or the other person's car! So clean were both cars that the owner of the hit vehicle kept asking me if I was sure I had hit his car. After which he said to me in front of the small crowd that had gathered, "I don't know which God you serve, but keep serving Him for HE is miraculous!" His words jolted back to memory my challenge to God earlier that month, "Prove to me that paying tithe is necessary." This was my proof! I chose to honour God with my tithe, and HE saved me from having to pay for damages twice the amount of the cost of my car!

Believers, always remember, you can never outgive God. Also, giving to God is always a gain and never a loss! Honour Him with your tithes.

3. Give Offerings

Offerings differ from tithes. Unlike a tithe, which is the first 10% of your income, an offering speaks to any additional amount you give after that. An offering is also usually left up to your discretion and reflects any amount you feel led to give at any particular moment. Every now and then, give a sacrificial offering, one that seriously stretches your faith.

I remember my finances being very low due to numerous expenses one particular month. Things were so low I was not sure how I was going to even fill my gas tank without having to touch my savings. I had only one thousand Jamaican dollars left for offering, which I had divided out for the rest of the month. One night, while at church, the usual call was made for offering, and I took out two hundred dollars to place in the offering box. However, on my way to give, I heard my Bishop say to the audience, "People of God, give more than what is in your hand; give the best of what is in your purse or wallet." My knees immediately felt weak because all I had in my purse that night was the one thousand dollar offering that was to serve me for the whole month. My Bishop was not addressing me in particular, but I felt so convicted. After much conviction, I returned to my seat, removed the remaining eight hundred dollars, and proceeded to give all of my monthly offering at once. All I said was, "God, I am trusting You." Two days later, a friend visited my home, handed me an envelope, and said, "Here, I felt led to bless you with some gas for your car." I opened the envelope to find ten thousand dollars, exactly ten times more than what I had placed in the offering box just the night before! I never discussed with anyone that my car needed gas but look at God! "Give, and it will be given to you. A good measure, pressed down, shaken together and running over, will be poured into your lap. For with the measure you use, it will be measured to you." (Luke 6:38 – KJV).

4. Help the Needy

Proverbs 14:31 says, "Whoever oppresses the poor shows contempt for their Maker, but whoever is kind to the needy honors God." (NIV). When I saw this scripture for the first time, it was quite an eye-opener because it implies that if I mistreat the needy, then I am showing disdain for my Creator. However, when I serve and show kindness to those in need, I am honouring God.

Many times our attitude towards the poor can be rather unkind, especially when they seek our help. We speak negative things about them, roll up our car windows when they approach us, hold our heads straight when we pass them on the street or throw coins at them in scorn when and if we decide to give to them. I readily admit that it used to be such a great source of frustration for me encountering someone begging seemingly at every other stoplight. Not to mention some of them were rather aggressive and seemingly unprincipled. However, we must come to a place where our giving is no longer about us but it is out of love and respect for God and our fellow man. Doing God's will willingly is proof of our love for Him. Showing compassion to the poor is also an indication that the love of God is in us (See 1 John 3:17).

Let us become intentional about seeking out less fortunate persons in our everyday life to bless. It does not necessarily have to be with physical money but with our substance. Daily, you can choose to bless a stranger or even someone you are acquainted with. We can bless someone with food who is without. What if someone only has one pair of shoes that is damaged, but you have several; you can bless them with a pair or more from yours. The way we use our money can be a form of discipleship. When we meet someone's physical needs, it opens the door to allow us to address their spiritual needs. I have personally found that when I am kind to some of the windscreen wipers on the street, they welcome conversation that allows me to minister to them. Loving God means loving people. Loving people requires us to show compassion and share through our giving. When we give towards the physical needs of others, let us also show love by addressing their spiritual needs as well.

Tip: Start very simple. Step up your offerings to keep building your faith.

Prayer

Lord, bless me so I can be a blessing to Your kingdom and a blessing to others. May I never appear before the LORD empty-handed, but may I give as I am able, according to the blessing the LORD, my God, has given me. May I never get weary in well doing, nor faint in doing so, that in due season, I shall reap. Amen.

HOLY SPIRIT DEPENDENCE

Trust in the Lord with all thine heart; and lean not unto thine own understanding. In all thy ways acknowledge him, and he shall direct thy paths.
Proverbs 3:5-6 – KJV

Chapter 10
Holy Spirit Dependence

Some time ago, one of my lecturers in Bible school showed our class an effective demonstration of trust in the following way. He blindfolded one of my fellow classmates and instructed him to make his way to the back of the room. Sir advised the young gentleman that he would lead him safely to his destination by providing him only with audible directions. The room had several concrete columns, so if the young man did not keenly follow our lecturer's instructions, he could easily have a very painful collision in any one of those columns. The lecturer began to instruct him when to go left, when to go right, straight ahead and when to stop. After a few near misses from heading headfirst into one of the concrete columns, he eventually made his way safely to the back of the room. The point of the exercise was to prove that fulfilling our Godly destiny requires us to trust and obey the voice of God (through His Word and Holy Spirit), to determine our direction and lead us toward that desired direction. This requires us to walk by faith and not by sight.

As a new believer, one of the first things you need to learn is how to move from a life of self-reliance to one that rests totally in the wisdom of God. If we are to live in victory, we must make Jesus Christ Lord over every area of our lives. We must follow Him in faith just as sheep follow a shepherd confidently, trusting him solely for their protection, provision, and direction.

Trusting God with our whole heart means we have an unwavering confidence in His sovereignty over us, His ability to direct our lives and to fulfill that which He has promised concerning us. We demonstrate our trust in Him through consistent and perfect obedience to His Word; that is, acknowledging and doing exactly as His Word says. Jesus says in John 14:15, if we love Him, we will keep His commandments. He goes on further to say in John 15:14 that we are His friends if we do that which He has commanded. In other words, this kind of faith builds intimacy with God. As this intimacy grows, we learn more about Him, and then He begins to reveal more about Himself and His plans to us. We become more keen to the sound of His voice and directives, thus allowing us to grow in wisdom and understanding. Therefore, the habit of trusting or building our faith produces glorious rewards and is a vital key if we are to grow in God. No wonder Hebrews 11:6a says, "Without faith, it is impossible to please Him." (KJV).

Our trust in God that leads to obedience is what enables us as Christians to live above sin. The degree to which we can successfully live above sin is a vivid indication of our level of spiritual growth. Obedience to the Word of God is vital because it has the ability to determine our destiny; that is, it could be a matter of life and death. I learned this very costly lesson in 2019 when the motor vehicle I was driving ended up in a collision with a truck.

One Sunday morning, on my way home from church, I suddenly began to experience an overwhelming sense of physical weariness. My eyelids began to feel heavy as if I was about to fall asleep while driving. I began to pray relentlessly, asking the Lord to take my brother and I safely home. After reaching less than five minutes away from home, I remember becoming annoyed as the red light caught me at the last stoplight before home. As I came to a halt behind a white box truck, I had my right foot on the brake and the vehicle still in drive as I waited. Immediately, I felt a tugging within, and a still small voice said, "Put the vehicle in park until the light changes." The voice was so clear, but I ignored it. I figured I was too tired to even put the vehicle in park; I just wanted to get home. Seconds after, I heard the sound of my brother's voice screaming out my name. When my eyes snapped open, it was just in time to see my car traversing headlong into the box truck in front of us. It was too late; somehow, in those few seconds after hearing and ignoring that still, small voice I had fallen asleep, my foot slipped off the brake, and we ended up colliding into the back of the truck.

Having seen the damage to my car, many, including the truck driver, were amazed that my brother and I never got a scratch. Thankfully, the truck only suffered a broken taillight; my car, on the other hand, was not as well-off. My insurance did not cover all the cost for the damage; my insurance premium went through the roof, the value of my fairly new car depreciated significantly, I had to pay for taxis to move around and my car was out of commission for over six months; that is, half of the year! I could have saved all that money and avoided that accident altogether had I been obedient to the still small voice of the Holy Spirit.

Tip: Delayed Obedience is Disobedience.

Bonus Tip: Make a habit of consulting your Heavenly Father concerning all your daily decisions and make a concerted effort to walk in obedience to His Word.

Conclusion

One of the primary lessons of this book is that after becoming a new believer, our ultimate aim is to grow up in God. The speed with which we are able to achieve this will be largely dependent on our level of hunger and intentionality in actively pursuing God and working on our relationship with Him. Spiritual acceleration requires deliberate action and work.

There are two main steps that will enable us to achieve this effectively: we must throw out the trash and then feed from the Living Tree. This entails disposing of those old Possessions, Practices, Personality traits, People, and Pursuits that either pose a threat to or negatively affect our relationship with God and replacing them with new and edifying ones that will enable us to accelerate spiritually and successfully begin to grow up in God. This is the process of transforming our minds more in line with the mind of Christ. This transformation can be achieved by addressing five major areas in our lives through the acronym B.I.R.T.H.:

- Books – Reading the right ones.
- Individuals – Connecting with the right ones.

- Routine Prayer – Scheduling our lives around our prayer life.
- Time, Talent, Treasures – Honouring God in these areas of our lives.
- Holy Ghost Dependence – Learning to rely on God rather than self.

When we apply all the above, it will enable us to have an encounter with God; that is, it will bring us to a greater place of intimacy with God. Only those who are desperate for God and seeking Him in like manner will be able to obtain this personal relationship. It is this intimacy that will cause us to hear from Him daily. It is this intimacy that will allow us to live an inspired Christian life. It is this intimacy that will sustain us and bring us through the difficult times in our journey. It is this intimacy that will enable us to bring other men to God and it is this intimacy that will ultimately lead us towards a heavenly eternity. This is my prayer for you, my beloved.

I love you. Be blessed and continue to grow up in God!

Final Message From The Author

When it comes on to accelerating spiritually, everyone's journey is somewhat unique. However, each one can learn from someone else's journey. There are general principles.

The principles in this book cover lessons that I learned and am learning from my journey toward spiritual maturity. They have worked amazingly for me and others I have shared them with when applied correctly. I deliberately kept them simple and practical so they can be easily applied. The book has been structured in such a way that you can easily follow and apply for quick results in record time. As you engage in your own journey, you may also discover additional principles that work. Write them down, use them and share them.

We are all in this together. It is important for us to share knowledge among ourselves as kingdom people because through knowledge, the just are delivered (See Proverbs 11:9).

I am so grateful to you for reading this manual to the end. I pray that it stirs up a fire in you to pursue God like never before. In applying its content, may you experience an encounter with God that changes your life forever. May you continually be inspired. I declare that you will experience a divine shift that will transform your entire life and catapult you into direct alignment with the purpose and will of God for your life.

In the proceeding 31-day journal, please record daily how you have applied the various keys in this book to your daily life and give a progress report on how they have been helping you to grow up in God. Feel free to email me a testimonial at sherinehemmings84@gmail.com.

Blessings always,
Sherine
Your Spiritual Acceleration Trainer

Day 1

Day 2

_____

_____

_____

_____

_____

_____

_____

_____

_____

_____

_____

_____

_____

_____

_____

_____

_____

_____

_____

Day 3

Day 4

Day 5

Day 6

Day 7

Day 8

Day 9

Day 10

Day 11

Day 12

Day 13

Day 14

_____

_____

_____

_____

_____

_____

_____

_____

_____

_____

_____

_____

_____

_____

_____

_____

_____

_____

_____

Day 15

Day 16

_____

_____

_____

_____

_____

_____

_____

_____

_____

_____

_____

_____

_____

_____

_____

_____

_____

_____

_____

_____

_____

Day 17

Day 18

_____

_____

_____

_____

_____

_____

_____

_____

_____

_____

_____

_____

_____

_____

_____

_____

_____

_____

_____

Day 19

Day 20

_____

_____

_____

_____

_____

_____

_____

_____

_____

_____

_____

_____

_____

_____

_____

_____

_____

_____

_____

Day 21

Day 22

Day 23

Day 24

Day 25

Day 26

Day 27

Day 28

Day 29

_____

_____

_____

_____

_____

_____

_____

_____

_____

_____

_____

_____

_____

_____

_____

_____

_____

_____

_____

Day 30

Day 31